SCHOLASTIC

COUNTRY REPORT PROJECTS
FOR ANY COUNTRY

Ready-to-Go Templates and Easy Instructions for
26 Engaging Projects That Showcase Students' Learning

by Michael Gravois

New York • Toronto • London • Auckland • Sydney
Mexico City • New Delhi • Hong Kong • Buenos Aires

Teaching Resources

∿ DEDICATION ∿

To nieces and nephews in every country,
especially Jessica Ard, Wayne Ard, Carly Roth,
Kyle Gravois, Logan Gravois,
Rebeccah Sykes, Rachael Sykes, Robyn Sykes,
and Michael Joseph Mermel-Klein

Cover design by Maria Lilja
Interior design by Michael Gravois
Illustrations by Jim Palmer

ISBN 0-439-51887-3

2 3 4 5 6 7 8 9 10   40   10 09 08 07 06 05

~ TABLE OF CONTENTS ~

~ INTRODUCTION ~

It takes all sorts of people to make a world.
—Douglas Jerrold (1803–1857)

I am a citizen of the world.
—Diogenes Laërtius (3rd century)

The world is full of microcosms, each of which thrive unto themselves, boasting unique cultures, languages, and terrains. But the world is interdependent as well, with countries relying on their neighbors for trade and commerce, security, and the sharing of knowledge and ideas. By studying the diverse peoples that make up its citizenry, we not only gain a greater understanding of the world, but of ourselves as well.

The hands-on projects in this book are organized around a common theme—studying the countries of the world. They approach the topic from a variety of perspectives and are meant to help you tap into the individual strengths of students and help them form a bridge of knowledge between the cultures, making the world seem more accessible. These unique reports will inspire kids to learn more about the diverse countries on this planet, helping them to become better citizens of the world.

To tie your curriculum together, you can spread the activities throughout the subject areas. In math, you can study the economies of the world, creating pictographs of the goods and services that bolster a country's economy (page 9). In language arts, you can learn about folk tales that were passed down through generations of different cultures (page 52). In science, you can explore the indigenous plants and animals that are found in other regions of the world (pages 26 and 48). Integrate poetry and music into the social studies curriculum by having students report on unique musical instruments from different countries (page 51). Tap into the artistic intelligence of your class as they study the lives and styles of famous artists (page 60). Spotlight popular sports and games from other countries in your physical education classes (page 21). But above all, use the activities in this book to add a sense of fun to your classroom. Varying the types of activities in which your students are engaged keeps their school days interesting, challenging, and fun. And a classroom in which students enjoy themselves is a classroom where learning is taking place.

~ NATIONAL TREASURE CHEST ~

Student archaeologists will unearth a bounty of knowledge
while creating these chests filled with national treasures.

Materials

- scissors
- glue
- different-colored construction paper
- colored markers and pencils
- various craft materials
- index cards
- shoe boxes (one for each student)

Getting Started

A couple of weeks before starting this project, ask students to bring in shoe boxes.

How-To's

1. Encourage each student to choose a different country of the world. Tell students that they will create a treasure chest filled with objects representative of the country they chose.

2. Give each student a shoe box. Ask them to use different-colored construction paper to make the box's lid look like the national flag of the country.

3. Challenge students to collect, create, or draw objects that represent aspects of the country's topography, culture, cuisine, economy, flora, fauna, government, sports, art forms, people, religion, history, costume, ceremonies, and so on. Ask each student to collect at least six items.

4. For each item, ask students to write a paragraph on an index card, describing the object's significance.

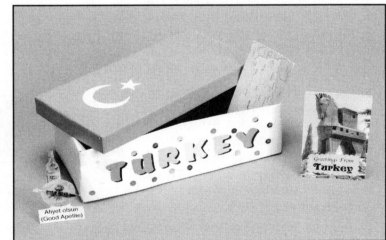

5. Have students place the objects and cards into the treasure chest. Then invite each student to give a short oral report on their selected country by opening the chest, revealing each item to the class, and explaining its importance.

~ REGIONAL WEB SITE ~

Integrate technology into your curriculum by having students create "Web sites" featuring their country's relationships with its neighbors.

Materials

- white construction paper
- glue sticks
- colored markers and pencils
- strips of bulletin board paper (3 feet long)
- yarn

Getting Started

Show students examples of Web sites on the Internet and demonstrate how home pages allow you to click on areas that link to related pages.

Describe the difference between visible and invisible borders of countries. Some borders—or political boundaries—can be seen, such as those that lie along coasts, rivers, or lakes. Others are lines that are marked on maps but invisible in the real world, such as those between neighboring states or countries.

How-To's

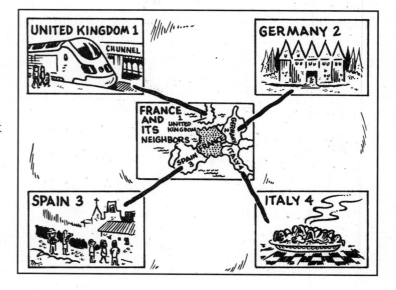

1. Ask students to use a sheet of construction paper to create a home page for the country they are studying. Have them draw a map of the country and its neighbors, including adjacent countries and bodies of water. Ask students to give the home page a title and number, and label all countries and bodies of water.

2. For each neighboring country, have students create a linking page that includes information about its relationship to the featured country. Make sure students give each page the same number they've assigned it on the home page. Linking pages that show neighboring countries should detail their political and cultural influences on the featured country. Linking pages that focus on bodies of water should describe their importance to the country.

3. For a thorough study of the region, you might ask students to include more detailed information on the linking pages, describing major cities and landforms, historical time lines, political figures, and so on.

4. Give each student a strip of bulletin board paper. Have them glue the home page in the center of the paper. Then have them glue the linking pages around the home page and run a length of yarn from each link to its corresponding section of the home page. Display the Web sites in the hall or around the classroom.

~ Economy Pictograph ~

Pictographs provide a quick and easy visual guide to a country's economic strengths.

Materials

- construction paper
- colored markers and pencils
- glue sticks
- scissors
- computer clip art *(optional)*

Getting Started

Help students understand the nature of a country's economy by discussing the economy of your own state. Challenge students to name goods and services that bring money into your state's economy. Write these items on the board, adding to the list if necessary. Ask students to suggest a simple icon that could be drawn to represent each item on the list (for example, an ear of corn could represent "produce" and a suitcase could represent "tourism").

How-To's

1. Have students conduct research on the major goods and services that bolster the economy of the country they're studying. Encourage them to find out how much money each item adds to the country's annual economy.

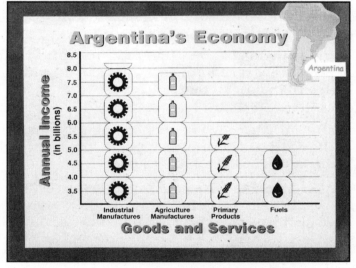

2. Ask students to create a 1-inch square icon for each item. You might also allow students to find icons in a clip-art program on your classroom computer.

3. Ask students to use these icons to create a pictograph of the country's economy. Have students title the graph, (Name of country)'s Economy. Label the *y* axis (left-hand side) Annual Income. The *x* axis (bottom) should be titled Goods and Services. (See the sample pictograph above.)

4. Above Goods and Services have students write the names of five goods/services that the country provides. Above each of these names ask students to stack copies of the 1-inch icons so that the stack reaches the line on the graph corresponding to the dollar amount that good or service brings to the economy. (Note: Some icons may have to be cut down in size to match the dollar amount.)

5. After students have glued their icons in place, display the pictographs on a bulletin board. Add a banner that reads, Money Makes the World Go 'Round.

~ PUZZLE TIME LINE ∿

Students will enjoy piecing together a country's history
with this unique time line activity.

Materials

- copies of Puzzle templates (pages 11–13)
- colored markers and pencils
- tape
- scissors

Getting Started

This activity provides the perfect opportunity for your school librarian to discuss research methods with your class. The librarian can introduce students to almanacs, book indexes, Internet search engines, and subject catalogs.

How-To's

1. Invite each student to choose a country. Ask students to conduct research on the history of that country. Allow them to use books (such as almanacs and textbooks) and computer technology (such as Encarta and Internet search engines).

2. As they conduct their research, ask students to write a list of key events from the country's history, starting with the earliest days of the country's founding up to the present. In note form, students should write the date of the events and a sentence describing each event.

3. Then ask them to choose the five most important events from their list. Give each student one copy of Puzzle templates 1 and 3 and three copies of Puzzle template 2. Have students complete a puzzle piece for each of the five events, following the directions at the top of the page.

4. After students have completed the pieces, have them cut out the pieces and tape them from behind into one long strip. Have students write the name of the country on a long strip of paper. Display the time lines and the title strips on a wall or bulletin board.

55,000 B.C.
Hunters and gatherers were the first people in Greece during the Old Stone Age.

404 B.C.
Great philosophers like Plato, Socrates, and Aristotle thrived during the Hellenistic period.

21st Century
Today, tourists visit the ruins of great structures that were built in Greece during ancient times.

~ PUZZLE TEMPLATE 1 ~

- Use this template for the first date in your time line.
- Print the date on the top line of the puzzle piece and write a sentence describing the event on the lines below.
- In the white space, draw a picture depicting the event.
- When you're done, cut out the puzzle piece.
- Tape this piece to the other puzzle pieces, sticking the tape at the back. When you look at the time line the earliest date should be on the left.

Country Report Projects for Any Country Scholastic Teaching Resources

~ Puzzle Template 2 ~

- Use this template for the middle three dates in your time line.
- Print the date on the top line of the puzzle piece and write a sentence describing the event on the lines below.
- In the white space, draw a picture depicting the event.
- When you're done, cut out the puzzle piece.
- Tape this piece to the other puzzle pieces, sticking the tape at the back. When you look at the time line the earliest date should be on the left.

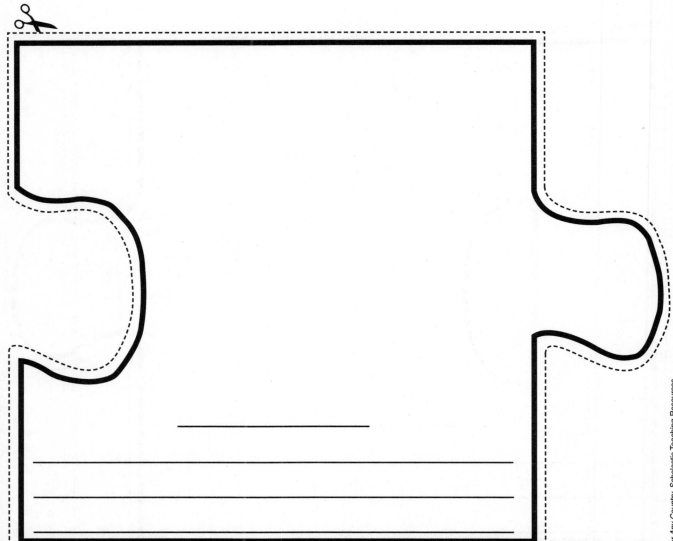

~ PUZZLE TEMPLATE 3 ~

- Use this template for the last date in your time line.
- Print the date on the top line of the puzzle piece and write a sentence describing the event on the lines below.
- In the white space, draw a picture depicting the event.
- When you're done, cut out the puzzle piece.
- Tape this piece to the other puzzle pieces, sticking the tape at the back. When you look at the time line the earliest date should be on the left.

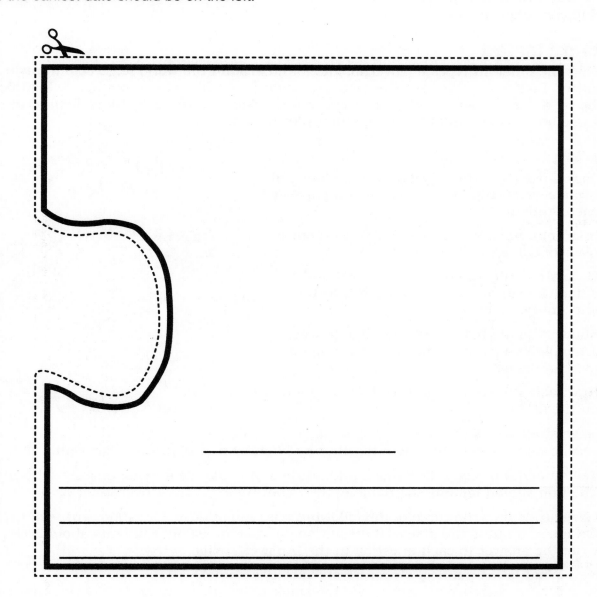

Country Report Projects for Any Country Scholastic Teaching Resources

∿ POLITICAL DATADISK ∿

Students explore the political structures of the world
as they collect data on the governments of different countries.

Materials

- copies of the Datadisk template (page 15)
- colored markers and pencils
- oaktag or construction paper
- scissors
- metal brads
- glue sticks

Getting Started

Discuss the different types of governments found around the world (e.g., communism, socialism, fascism, dictatorship, democracy, monarchy, oligarchy, republic). Ask students to choose a country and conduct research on its political structure. Allow them to use resource books and the Internet to gather information.

How-To's

1. Pass out a copy of the Datadisk template and two pieces of oaktag (or construction paper) to each student.

2. Instruct students to glue the disk onto one piece of oaktag.

3. Have students cut out the perimeter of the datadisk (without cutting out the Question and Answer spaces).

4. Show students how to use the datadisk as a template to cut a circle out of the second piece of oaktag.

5. Next, ask students to cut out the Q and A spaces on the first disk.

6. Have students place the Q and A datadisk over the second circle and fasten them together by pushing a brad through the center dot.

7. Tell students to write their name and a title on the datadisk using creative lettering. The title should include the name of their country (e.g., THE GOVERNMENT OF ITALY).

8. Have students write three of the following questions in the "Question" space of their datadisk, rotating the disk 1/3 revolution for each question. Students should then write the answer to each question in the "Answer" space.

   - What is the political structure of (country's name)?
   - Who is the current leader/administrator of (country's name)? Describe him/her.
   - How often does the leadership change? How are new leaders determined?
   - What are the different branches of its government?
   - Describe the different political parties of (country's name).

∿ Datadisk Template ∿

- Glue the disk onto a piece of oaktag and cut out the perimeter of the datadisk.
- Use the datadisk as a template to cut a circle out of the second piece of oaktag.
- Cut out the Question and Answer spaces on the first disk.
- Place the Q and A datadisk over the blank circle and fasten them together by pushing a brad through the center dot.
- Write a title for the datadisk using creative lettering and draw a related illustration.
- Write your questions in the question space and your answers in the answer space, rotating the datadisk each time.

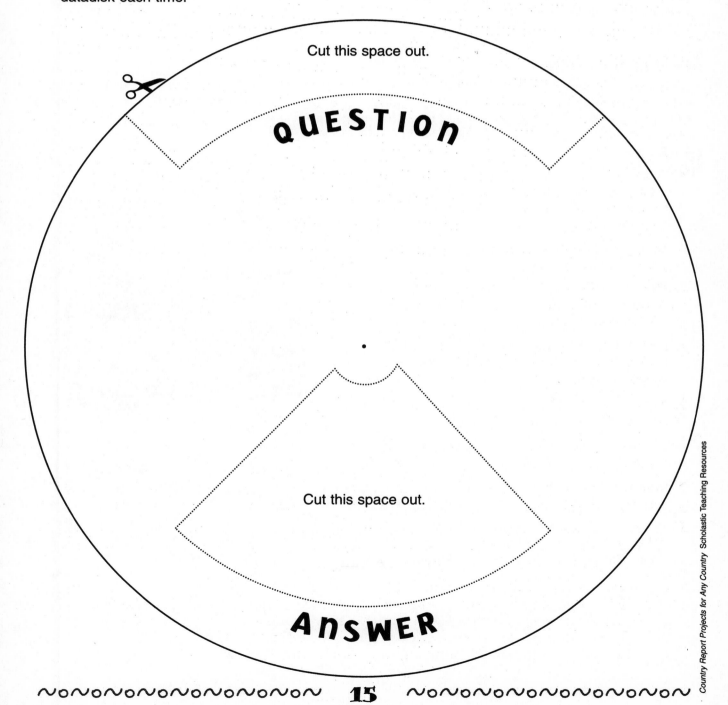

Country Report Projects for Any Country Scholastic Teaching Resources

∿ PAPER-DOLL COSTUMES ∿

Students can learn a lot about the diversity of the world
by studying the traditional costumes of different cultures.

Materials

- copies of the Paper-Doll template (page 17)
- colored markers and pencils
- oaktag or poster board
- scissors
- craft materials
- construction paper

Getting Started

Share some examples of paper-doll clothing patterns with students to give them ideas for
this project that features the traditional clothing of different cultures. Pattern books can
be found at your local library.

How-To's

1. Give each student a copy of the
   Paper-Doll template. Have students
   cut out the figures.

2. Ask them to trace the edges of the
   paper dolls onto a sheet of oaktag or
   poster board and cut out the figures
   again. (Students can share templates
   if you'd like.)

3. Encourage students to use construction
   paper and craft materials to dress their
   paper dolls in the traditional clothing of
   a man and woman from the country
   they are studying.

4. In the box below the figures, have
   students write the name of the
   country represented, followed by
   a paragraph describing the native
   costumes that they created.

5. Finally, have students fold the paper
   dolls in half (like a book) so their faces
   meet. When they are reopened, the
   paper dolls can stand freely. Display
   everyone's paper dolls on a table or
   counter, and enjoy the diverse
   costumes of cultures found
   throughout the world.

GERMANY

Tracht is the German word for traditional
costume. Men wore pants called lederhosen
and bands above their calves. Hats often had
emblems or feathers.

~ Paper-Doll Template ~

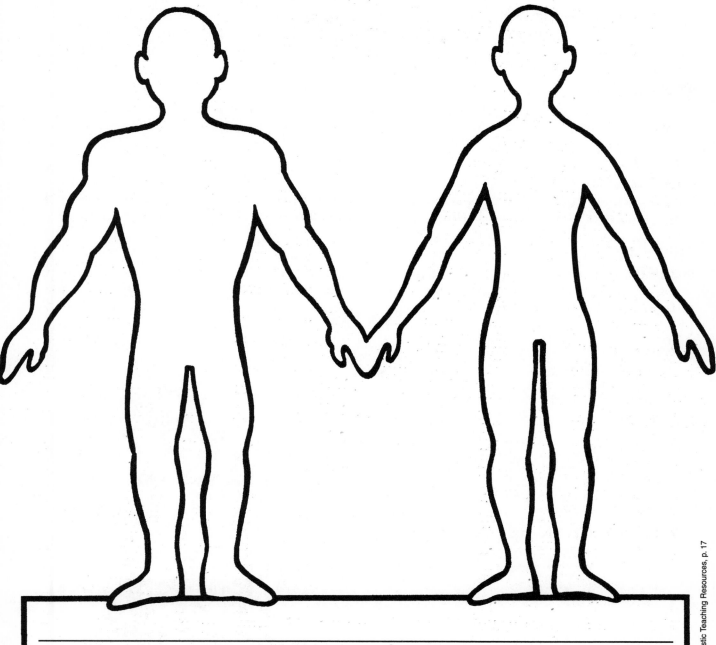

_____

_____

_____

_____

_____

Country Report Projects for Any Country Scholastic Teaching Resources, p. 17

∿ FAMOUS PEOPLE BOOK ∿

Students learn about the contributions of famous people from different countries as they create People Books.

Materials

- Graphic Organizer (page 20)
- colored markers and pencils
- white construction paper
- craft materials
- scissors
- glue sticks

Getting Started

Invite each student to choose a different country. Then have students research the life of a famous—or infamous—person from that country. Encourage them to consider political figures, entertainers, artists, scientists, humanitarians, athletes, and historical figures.

How-To's

Give each student a copy of the graphic organizer to record information about the famous person he or she is researching. Students can use this data to write the paragraphs inside their completed People Books.

TO CREATE A FEMALE PEOPLE BOOK:

1. Fold a sheet of white construction paper in half horizontally twice and then once vertically.

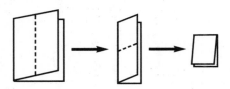

2. Open it to reveal eight panels.

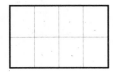

3. Cut the bottom left and bottom right panels along the dotted lines. Save the two scraps of paper.

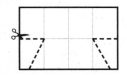

HENRY VIII

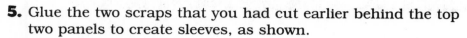

4. Fold in the top left and top right panels.

5. Glue the two scraps that you had cut earlier behind the top two panels to create sleeves, as shown.

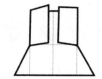

6. Add a head, legs, and hands to the figure.

7. Use buttons, markers, fabrics, dimensional glue, and other craft materials to decorate the figure. Create clothing that is representative of the famous person.

8. Using construction paper, create an object to put in the person's hand that is relevant to his or her accomplishment.

9. Inside the two flaps write two complete, detailed paragraphs describing the significance and the accomplishments of the person.

10. Prepare an oral report on this person to present to the class.

TO CREATE A MALE PEOPLE BOOK:

1. Repeat steps 1 and 2 of the Female People Book directions.

2. Cut the bottom left and bottom right panels as indicated below, and make a slit up the center to create pants.

3. Glue the two scraps of paper that you had cut behind the top two panels to create sleeves.

4. Repeat steps 6 to 10 of the Female People Book directions.

After students have completed their reports, staple the arms and legs of the People Books to a bulletin board. Add a banner that reads, LIFE IS AN OPEN BOOK.

~ Graphic Organizer ~

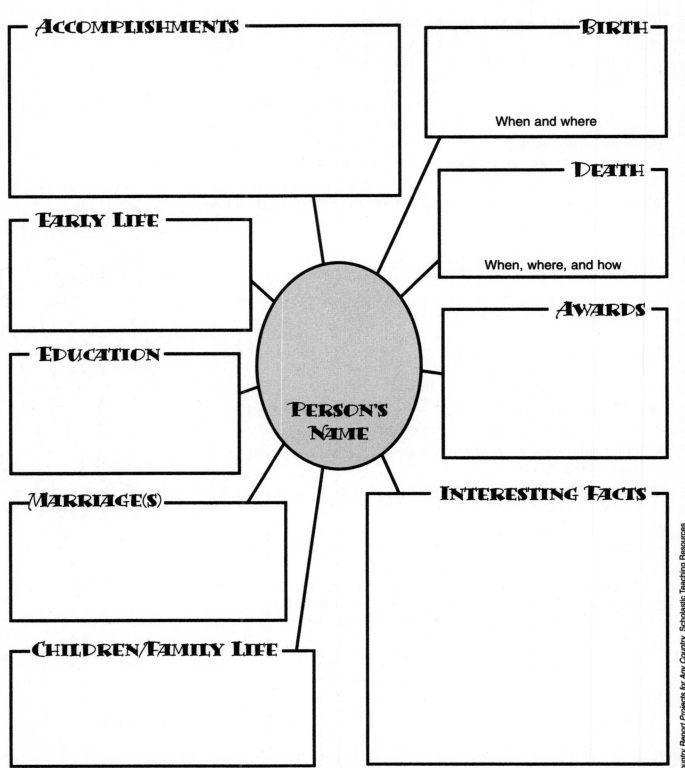

ACCOMPLISHMENTS

BIRTH

When and where

EARLY LIFE

DEATH

When, where, and how

EDUCATION

AWARDS

PERSON'S NAME

MARRIAGE(S)

INTERESTING FACTS

CHILDREN/FAMILY LIFE

Country Report Projects for Any Country Scholastic Teaching Resources

~ WIDE WORLD OF SPORTS ~

Surround your classroom with a parade of colorful banners
that spotlight popular sports and games from other countries.

Materials
- bulletin board paper in different colors
- colored markers and pencils
- scissors
- white construction paper
- glue sticks

Getting Started
As a warm-up for this activity, take your students outside and allow them to play a favorite sport or game. When you return to class have students research sports that are popular in other countries.

How-To's

1. Cut strips of bulletin board paper into 5-foot lengths. For variety, use several colors of bulletin board paper.

2. Turn each strip into two banners by cutting a V-shaped line across the middle of the paper, as shown.

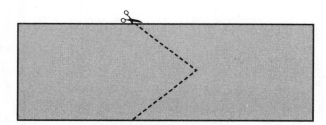

3. Ask each student to select a different country and to research a popular sport or game that is played in that country.

4. On a square sheet of white construction paper, have students draw a picture of the sport being played. Have them glue the picture near the top of the banner.

5. Have students write the name of the country where the sport is played above the illustration, and the name of the sport below the illustration.

6. On the back of the banner, invite students to write a couple of detailed paragraphs that describe the rules of the game, its origins, equipment used, and so on. Ask students to give an oral report on the sport they researched, holding the banner up as they speak.

7. Display the completed banners around the classroom to brighten the walls.

~ CULTURAL CUISINE PLACEMAT ~

Student "chefs" create a smorgasbord of colorful placemats
that highlight traditional foods from around the world.

Materials

- construction paper
- recipe books
- scissors
- glue sticks
- colored markers and pencils
- laminating machine (optional)

Getting Started

Ask your students to name foods that most people would consider traditional American fare (for example, hot dogs, hamburgers, or apple pie). Gather a selection of recipe books from the library that features foods from different countries. Add them to your class library for students to use as reference books.

How-To's

1. Give each student a few sheets of construction paper, as well as a large piece that can be used as the placemat.

2. Ask students to cut out letters from a sheet of construction paper to spell the name of the country on which they'll be reporting. Have them glue the name of the country across the top of their placemat.

3. Have students find recipes for some traditional foods from their chosen country. Have them copy the recipes and glue them to one side of their placemat.

4. Encourage students to create a construction-paper version of the meal and glue that to the placemat. Have them add utensils and a napkin to the side of the plate.

5. Next, tell them to create a glass from construction paper. On the side of the glass they should write the name and recipe of a traditional drink from their country. Have them glue the glass to their placemat.

6. Laminate the placemats, if possible. Students can then use the placemats for the rest of the year during lunch time or snack time. You could also use them as a decorative bulletin board that features foods from around the world.

7. As a culminating activity, invite parents to cook their child's recipe. Students can bring samples of the different foods to class, and you can host an international buffet where everyone can sample the tastes of different cultures.

~ Architectural Relief ~

Turn your students into architects by having them construct
3-D renderings of unique building designs found in other countries.

Materials

- glue sticks or spray glue
- 8½-by-11-inch copy paper
- colored markers or pencils
- thin black markers
- scissors
- oaktag

Getting Started

Show students examples of building designs by American architects, such as Frank Lloyd Wright, and examples of famous skyscrapers, such as the Empire State Building, to help oil their creativity for this three-dimensional, hands-on project.

How-To's

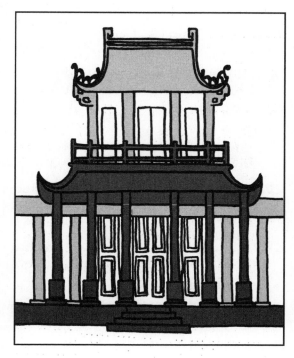

1. Ask students to research architectural designs that are unique to the country they're studying (e.g., pagodas in Japan, onion domes in Russia, thatched huts in Tahiti).

2. On sheets of copy paper, have students draw a picture of a building or home from the country they chose. Guide them to think about things that might be seen in the foreground (such as landscaping or roofs), the midground (such as columns or balconies), and the background (such as the main structure of the building). Ask them to first draw the picture in pencil, outline it with a black marker, and then erase the stray pencil marks. (In the example at right, the white objects will appear in the background; the light gray objects will appear in the midground; and the dark gray objects will appear in the foreground. See the photograph of the final project on page 25.)

3. Make three copies of the picture that each student drew.

4. Have students use glue sticks or spray glue to attach one copy to a sheet of oaktag. This will make the picture sturdier. Have students color the picture using markers or colored pencils.

5. On a second copy of the picture, have students color the objects that will appear in the foreground and midground of the picture. Tell students to cut out these items, glue them onto oaktag, and then cut them out again. If two or more objects overlap, students should cut them out as a single piece. (Note: The foreground objects in this layer will serve as a base on which students can glue the final layer in step 9. This way, the foreground objects in step 9 will pop out from the midground layer.)

6. To make these midground items pop out, affix them to the main picture with small tabs. Have students cut out several dozen 1" x $\frac{1}{4}$" strips of oaktag. Fold the small strips in half and then in half again, creating three creases with four small panels (see below). Tear off one of the small panels on the strips, leaving three panels (with two folds).

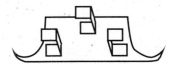

7. Have students fold these tabs into brackets, put some glue on one end of each bracket, and affix the brackets to the backs of the objects that will appear in the midground (see below). Glue several brackets onto each object to give it support, varying the direction in which each bracket faces. Glue the other end of the brackets to the background picture so the midground objects pop out.

8. On the third copy of the picture, have students color the objects that will appear in the foreground. Have them cut out these objects, glue them onto oaktag, and then cut them out again.

9. Have students glue brackets to these foreground objects, then glue them onto the tops of the midground layer so the objects pop out into the foreground. The picture will now have three layers—a background, a midground, and a foreground.

10. Have students glue the completed picture onto a large sheet of oaktag or poster board, leaving a 2-inch border across the top and down the sides, and a 6-inch writing area at the bottom.

11. In the space above the picture have students use creative lettering to write the name of the country where this unique architecture can be found.

12. In the area below the picture instruct students to write a complete, detailed paragraph that describes the architectural style and its significance to the country where it is found.

13. Display the completed projects on a bulletin board. Add a banner that reads, OUTSTANDING ARCHITECTURE. Curve the banner in and out a few times to give it a wavy, three-dimensional effect. Tape the banner to the bulletin board wherever the banner touches the bulletin board.

CHINA

A pagoda is a building found on Buddhist temple grounds. It originated in India, but in the sixth century Buddhism and Buddhist architecture came to Japan or Korea, while it was coming through China. However, the shape of the pagoda changed from a dome to a several level structure. Because they had plenty of wood in China, they built beautifully designed pagodas from the wood.

~ INDIGENOUS ANIMALS MOBILE ~

Jazz up your classroom with colorful, spiral mobiles
that feature indigenous animals from distant countries.

Materials
- copies of the Mobile template (page 27)
- colored markers and pencils
- string
- scissors
- oaktag
- glue sticks

Getting Started

Have students research animals that are indigenous to the country that they are studying. Students should make a list of these animals, and then find books and Web sites that provide detailed information and pictures.

How-To's

1. Give each student a copy of the Mobile template and a sheet of oaktag. Ask students to use a glue stick to put a couple of light strokes of glue on the template and stick it to the oaktag. Have them cut out the spiral, then separate the two sheets, keeping the oaktag section.

2. Invite students to decorate the spiral, using colored pencils and markers.

3. Help students use the point of sharp scissors to poke five holes along the length of the spiral. Poke another hole through the center of the spiral.

4. Instruct students to thread a 10-inch piece of string through the center hole, tying a knot underneath to keep the string in place. When you hold the end of the string, the spiral should swirl downward.

5. Have students thread a 3-inch piece of string through each of the holes along the length of the spiral. Have students tie knots at the top of these strings to hold them in place and so that they hang below the spiral.

6. Encourage students to draw and color five indigenous animals they had researched. They should also create a mirror image of each of these animals. Then students can glue the mirror images back to back at the bottom of each piece of string that hangs down.

7. Finally, ask students to write the name of the country in which these animals can be found on two oaktag panels that each measure 4 inches by 2 inches. They should glue these panels back to back in the middle of the 10-inch support string.

8. Hang the spiral mobiles around the classroom, allowing them to spin freely.

~ Mobile Template ~

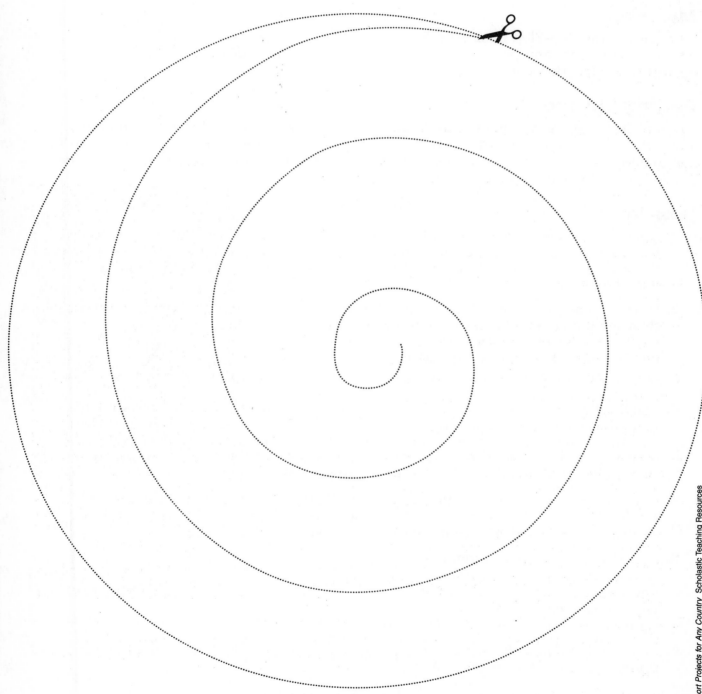

Country Report Projects for Any Country Scholastic Teaching Resources

~ CONTRASTING FLIP-FLOP BOOK ~

Help students learn more about foreign countries by exploring the ways they are different from our own country.

Materials

- copies of the Flip-Flop Book template (page 29)
- colored markers and pencils
- white construction paper
- scissors
- glue sticks

Getting Started

It is often easier for students to understand concepts with which they have no prior knowledge by first relating them to ideas with which they are familiar. This project asks students to discuss aspects of their own country and then describe how these aspects differ in the foreign country they're studying.

How-To's

1. Give each student a copy of the Flip-Flop Book template. Have students glue the template to a sheet of white construction paper. (This step is optional, but it keeps the writing from showing through the cover flaps and gives the project a more finished look.)

2. Have students cut each of the dashed lines on their templates, making sure to stop where the dashed line meets the solid line. Have them fold the flaps down so that the writing lines are on the inside of the fold (see right).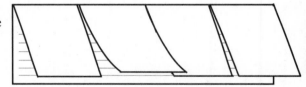

3. The flip-flop book now has four panels. On the cover of each panel, have students write the title of the aspects of the countries they will contrast (e.g., political structure, climate, economy, topography, flora, fauna, sports, population, religious structure, costume, cuisine, language, education, musical styles, folklore, culture, and so on). Under each title, ask students to draw a related icon or picture.

4. In the lower box inside each panel, have students write the name of the country they're studying. On the lines under the two boxes, have students write a few sentences comparing and contrasting the concept on the flap's cover.

5. If you would like your students to create a flip-flop book with more than four panels, simply have them tape two books together to create an eight-panel book.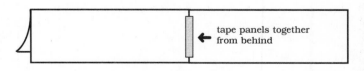

tape panels together from behind

6. After students have finished their flip-flop books, display the books on a bulletin board under a banner that reads, A WORLD OF DIFFERENCES.

The United States

(country)

The United States

(country)

The United States

(country)

The United States

(country)

∿ TOURIST SCRAPBOOK ∿

Send students on a virtual journey to distant lands
so they can collect mementos for their scrapbooks.

Materials

- copies of the Snapshot template (page 31)
- colored markers and pencils
- resealable plastic bags
- construction paper
- scissors
- glue sticks
- envelopes

Getting Started

Scrapbooking techniques can be used across the curriculum, encouraging students to record their learning in a hands-on, visually appealing way, while improving their organizational, writing, and artistic skills. Scrapbooking invites them to conceptualize an idea, organize their thoughts, and get their hands and minds actively involved in expressing these thoughts three-dimensionally.

How-To's

1. Give each student a sheet of construction paper (scrapbook page), a copy of the Snapshot template, and an envelope. Ask students to research a foreign country and create a scrapbook page filled with items they might collect if they could travel there.

2. Invite students to write a letter to a loved one back home describing the things they saw and did on their virtual trip, and put the letter in the envelope. Have them address the envelope, draw a stamp that reflects the country they "traveled" to, and attach the envelope to the scrapbook page.

3. Have students create souvenir objects (like ticket stubs, postcards, brochures, maps, and coins) and attach them to the scrapbook page. Three-dimensional objects can be placed in a resealable plastic bag and taped to the page. Have students write a sentence next to each object that explains its significance.

4. Students can use the snapshot template to draw "photographs" of sights they might have seen.

5. Display the scrapbook pages on a bulletin board under a banner that reads, [YOUR NAME]'S CLASS TRAVELS THE WORLD.

~ Snapshot Template ~

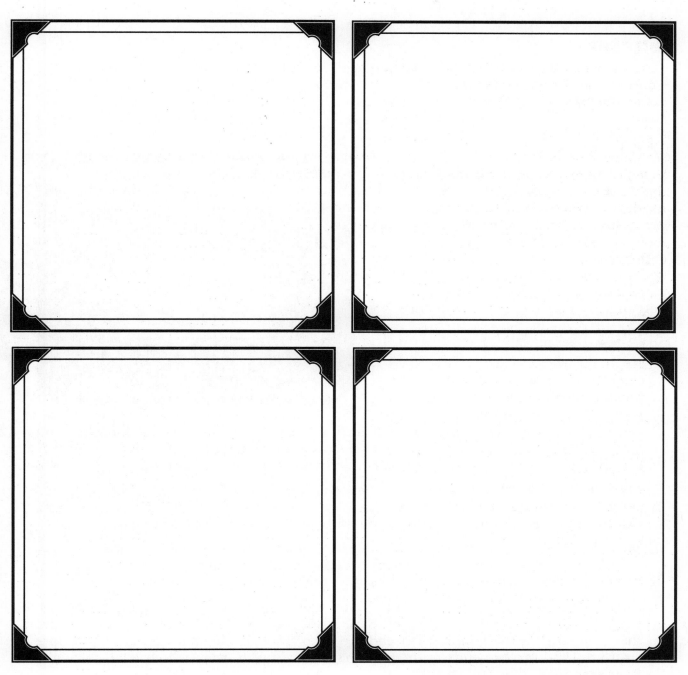

Country Report Projects for Any Country Scholastic Teaching Resources

∿ TOPOGRAPHY VIDEO BOOK ∿

Turn your students into documentarians and cinematographers
as they take their "video cameras" on geographical expeditions.

Materials

- copies of the Video Camera templates (pages 33-36)
- colored markers and pencils
- glue sticks or spray glue
- tape
- oaktag
- scissors
- craft sticks
- stapler

Getting Started

Video cameras are familiar recording devices to today's students. They are used to record everything from family vacations to television documentaries to motion pictures. Before starting this activity, show your students a video documentary that focuses on a specific place so they can get a sense of the language and style of a documentary.

Title: My Video Journey to Costa Rica
— by Jennifer Rubino

How-To's

1. Pass out one copy of the Film Strip template and two copies of the Writing Strip template to each student. Tell students that they will create six illustrations using the Film Strip template detailing topographical elements found in the country they're studying. The six panels should cover major landforms, waterways, deserts, forests, mountains, canyons, the predominant climate, and so on.

2. Have students write a descriptive paragraph on the Writing template to accompany each illustration. Encourage students to write the sentences in the first person, as if the videographer was talking about the image as he or she was filming it.

3. Next, hand out copies of the Video Camera templates. Have students follow the directions on the templates to cut out and assemble the video cameras. To make the camera pieces sturdier, have students glue them to a sheet of oaktag.

4. Ask students to cut out their writing strips, put them in order, and staple them to the video camera where indicated. Then have students cut out the film strip and, following the directions on the template, thread the strip through the camera. Have them tape craft sticks to the two ends of the film strip to prevent it from being pulled through the slots.

5. Display the video cameras on a bulletin board under the title THE WORLD'S BEST DOCUMENTARIES—ADMISSION FREE.

~ Video Camera Cover ~

1. Glue the video camera cover to a sheet of oaktag and cut it out.
2. Write your name and the title of your report in the rectangle at the top of the video camera. Use creative lettering.

Title:

~ Video Camera Interior ~

1. Glue the video camera interior to a sheet of oaktag and cut it out.
2. Tape the left edge of the cover to the left edge of the interior so it opens like a book.

Slot B

Cut slots A and B.
Thread your film strip through slot A from behind and down through slot B so only one frame can be seen at a time. Then tape each end tab to a craft stick to prevent the film from being pulled through.

Slot A

Place writing sheets here.

Put your writing sheets in order and staple the left edges so they cover these instructions.

~ Film Strips ~

After you thread your film strip through the camera, glue this tab to a craft stick.

After you thread your film strip through the camera, glue this tab to a craft stick.

Glue this tab behind panel 3.

~◦~◦~◦~◦~◦~◦~◦~◦~◦~◦~◦~◦~◦~◦~◦~◦~◦~◦~

~ WRITING STRIPS ~

Panel #   :

Panel #   :

Panel #   :

Panel #   :

~ LANDMARKS ACCORDION CASE ~

Invite students to explore and collect information
about famous landmarks and organize it in this handy carrying case.

Materials

- 18-by-12-inch construction paper
- 8½-by-11-inch white card stock
- colored markers and pencils
- glue sticks
- tape
- scissors

Getting Started

Show students pictures of famous landmarks in America, such as the Empire State
Building, the Golden Gate Bridge, the Alamo, and the Washington Monument. Discuss
their historical and cultural significance.

How-To's

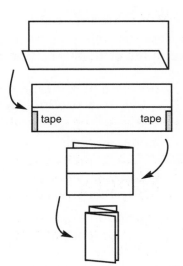

1. Give each student a sheet of 18-by-12-inch construction
   paper. Ask students to place it in front of them horizontally
   and fold up the bottom 4 inches, creating a long pocket.

2. Have students tape the two ends of the pocket closed.

3. Next, instruct them to fold the sheet in half so that the
   pocket is on the outside.

4. Then have them fold the two sides in half so that the
   pocket is on the inside of the accordion case.

5. Have students cut off the top 2 inches of the
   accordion case.

6. Next, have students cut the card stock in half, vertically
   and horizontally, to make four postcards.

7. On each postcard, have students draw a picture of an
   important landmark that can be found in the country
   they're studying. On the back of each card,
   encourage students to write a complete,
   detailed paragraph that describes the
   landmark's significance.

8. When they are finished, ask students
   to put each postcard into one of the
   pockets of the accordion case. Invite
   students to design a cover for their
   case that includes a title, such as
   FAMOUS LANDMARKS OF PERU.

~ Urban Advertisements Ꙩ

Your classroom will teem with mini ad agencies
as your students hone their powers of persuasion.

Materials

- Requirement Sheet (page 40)
- colored markers and pencils
- white construction paper
- tape recorder, blank tapes, and video camera *(optional)*
- 1 sheet of bulletin board paper (approximately 2 feet by 3 feet) for each group
- glue sticks
- old magazines
- rulers
- tape
- scissors

Getting Started

Have students look at ads in old magazines (travel magazines would be ideal). Ask them to find examples of ways advertisers try to entice readers into buying their product or visiting their destination.

Review the following propaganda techniques found in advertising. Ask students to find examples of these techniques in the magazine ads.

Bandwagon Technique—persuades people to buy a product by letting them know that other people are buying it

Testimonial/Transfer—uses the words (testimonial) or images (transfer) of famous people to persuade people to buy the product

Association—associates the product with fun times, patriotism, relaxation, or the like

Glittering Generalities—uses exaggerated, flowery words to describe a product

Repetition—repeats the product's name at least four times to make people remember it

Bait and Switch—entices consumers with a "FREE" offer, only to find out in the small print that they actually need four box tops, plus postage and handling

How-To's

1. Divide the class into groups of three or four and give each group a sheet of bulletin board paper (poster). Encourage each group to brainstorm about a foreign country or destination for which they will design an ad campaign. You might ask students to focus on major cities or capital cities of the world.

2. Ask students to decide who the *target audience* is for their product (e.g., children, adults, newlyweds, thrill-seekers) and discuss information about the destination that they feel should be mentioned in their advertising.

3. Distribute and review the Requirement Sheet with the class.

   To help with the television commercial part of this project, you might want to show examples of storyboards to your class. There are many examples on the Internet that you can find by typing "storyboard" into a search engine.

   Consider having students act out the radio and television ads for the class. You might want them to record the radio spots and television commercials. The class will enjoy hearing and watching themselves.

4. Encourage each group to decide which member(s) will be responsible for completing each element. Students can select jobs based on their talents. Copywriters can write the copy for the press release and for the radio spot. Art directors can design the visual components of the ads. Traffic managers can organize the workers so that everything is being completed in a timely fashion.

5. Students must share responsibility for completing the poster. Tell them that part of their final grade will be determined by how well they share in the production of the poster. If someone finishes his or her section of the poster, he or she should help the other members. Remind them that each member of the group is responsible for proof-reading *each* element of their project.

6. Invite the groups to present their campaigns to the class, reviewing and discussing each element of the project.

7. After the oral presentations, have groups glue their print ad, storyboard, and radio script to their poster.

8. Display the posters in the hall or on a class wall for everyone to see. Add a large banner that reads, TOURIST INFORMATION CENTER.

NOTE: If you would prefer your students to work individually, consider scaling back this project and asking each student to create only a print ad for his or her chosen destination.

~ Urban Advertisements ~
Requirement Sheet

TITLE

• Write the title of your destination across the top of your poster and list the complete name of each group member.

PRINT AD

• Design a magazine print ad for your destination on a piece of construction paper that measures at least $8\frac{1}{2}$ by 11 inches. Use one of the propaganda techniques discussed in class to help sell your product. Look at other magazine ads to get ideas.

• Add the title PRINT AD and attach the advertisement to your poster.

TELEVISION COMMERCIAL

• Write a television commercial for your destination that includes a different propaganda technique from the one used in the print ad.

• On a sheet of construction paper, create a storyboard for your commercial that shows the different camera angles used as well as the dialogue spoken by the actors or narrators. Each panel should be at least 5 inches square.

• Add the title TELEVISION COMMERCIAL and attach the storyboard to your poster.

RADIO SPOT

• Write the script for a 30- to 45-second radio commercial that includes a different propaganda technique from the ones used in the print ad or the television commercial.

• The script should include all the dialogue spoken by the actors and narrators. Note where music or sound effects are supposed to occur.

• Add the title RADIO SPOT and attach the script to your poster.

PRESS RELEASE

• Write a press release for your destination that could be sent to newspapers. The press release should contain a different propaganda technique from those already used.

• Add the title PRESS RELEASE and attach the press release to your poster.

Country Report Projects for Any Country Scholastic Teaching Resources

∿ FOREIGN LANGUAGE TRANSLATOR ∿

Students create Mini-Dictionaries of foreign words and phrases
to help them learn the "sounds" of other countries.

Materials
- colored markers and pencils
- scissors
- foreign language dictionaries
- copies of the Mini-Dictionary template (pages 42 and 43 copied double-sided)

Getting Started
Make double-sided copies of the Mini-Dictionary templates so that panel one appears directly behind the cover. Give one copy to each student, then demonstrate how to create the Mini-Dictionaries following the directions below.

How-To's

1. Cut the template in half along the dashed line.

2. Cut both sheets along the dotted lines. One sheet will have two slits, one at the top and one at the bottom. The other sheet will have an opening cut down the center of the fold (figure 1).

figure 1

3. Place the sheet with panels 3 and 6 faceup in front of you. Take the other sheet (the one with two cuts) and curl the sides of panel 1 into a cylinder and feed it through the hole in the first sheet (figure 2).

figure 2

4. Open up the sheets to lock the pages in place. Fold the pages into a book shape with the cover page on top. Make sure the pages are in the correct order (figure 3).

figure 3

5. Invite students to design a cover for their Mini-Dictionaries. Then ask them to follow the directions on each page to complete the Mini-Dictionaries.

6. Students can glue the Mini-Dictionaries into their notebooks to create an interactive notebook. Or you could post the Mini-Dictionaries on a bulletin board under a banner that reads, WORDS FOR THE WISE.

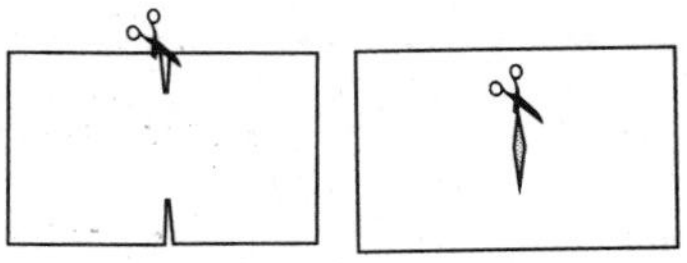

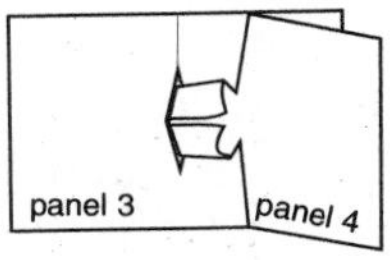

Write the foreign language equivalents
of the following words and phrases.

Hello.

_____

Good-bye.

_____

Good morning.

_____

Good afternoon.

_____

Good evening.

_____

Good night.

_____

1

Twenty _____

Thirty _____

Forty _____

Fifty _____

Sixty _____

Seventy _____

Eighty _____

Ninety _____

Hundred _____

Thousand _____

4

Write the foreign language words
of the following numbers.

One _____

Two _____

Three _____

Four _____

Five _____

Six _____

Seven _____

Eight _____

Nine _____

Ten _____

3

Draw an icon of four foods you might eat.
Write the foreign name of each.

6

Draw an icon of four things you might find in a classroom. Write the foreign name of each.

_____

_____

_____

_____

5

How are you?

_____

I'm fine.

_____

Thank you.

_____

You're welcome.

_____

Please.

_____

Excuse me.

_____

Back Cover

2

~ FESTIVAL OF KITES ~

Celebrate the festivals and holidays of other cultures
by creating this fanciful and high-flying bulletin board with your class.

Materials
- copies of the Kite template (page 45)
- blue and white bulletin board paper
- yarn
- scissors
- colored markers and pencils

Getting Started

Discuss the origins of American holidays such as the Fourth of July, Presidents' Day, Labor Day, Memorial Day, Thanksgiving, and Columbus Day. Explain the significance of the dates on which these holidays are celebrated and how these dates were decided upon.

How-To's

1. Give a copy of the Kite template to each student. Ask students to cut out the kite and bows.

2. Have students fold the four flaps along the dotted lines. Students will then have a kite with four flaps. Invite them to color the four flaps and use creative lettering to write the following titles on the tops of the flaps—HOLIDAY, ORIGIN, DATE, and DRAWING.

3. Have students fill in the following information under the appropriate flaps:

   Flap 1: Holiday Students should use creative lettering to write the name of the holiday on which they will be reporting.

   Flap 2: Origin Students should write a complete, detailed paragraph describing the origins of the holiday they chose.

   Flap 3: Date Students should write a few sentences about the date on which the holiday is celebrated and the significance of this date.

   Flap 4: Drawing Students should draw a picture related to this holiday.

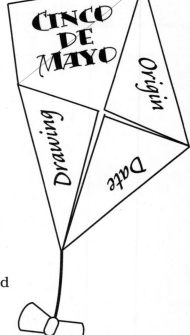

4. Give each student a length of yarn to use for the kite's tail. Have students color the bows, tape the yarn to the back of the kite, and tape the bows along the tail.

5. Use blue and white bulletin board paper to create a blue sky with white clouds on your bulletin board. Hang the kites in the paper sky to create an uplifting display.

~ Kite Template ~

Country Report Projects for Any Country Scholastic Teaching Resources

∾ CULTURE QUILT ∾

Turn a class wall into a large, colorful quilt
that highlights unique cultures throughout the world.

Materials
- copies of the Culture Quilt template (page 47)
- colored markers and pencils
- scissors
- tape

Getting Started

Show your students some examples of fabrics that feature a repetitive design to give students an idea for the "swatches" of fabric they will be creating for their culture quilts.

How-To's

1. Give each student a copy of the Culture Quilt template.

2. In the center square on the quilt, ask students to use creative lettering to write the name of the country they studied and their own name.

3. In the eight sections around the center square, students will create designs in repetitive patterns that illustrate an aspect of the country's culture. (For example, if a student were reporting on Mexico, one swatch could feature a repetitive pattern of sombreros and another could feature chili peppers.)

4. On the back of the quilt, encourage students to write a sentence about each of the swatches, describing the design's significance.

5. When they are done, ask students to cut out the quilt pattern.

6. Lay the patterns next to each other, facedown. Tape them from behind so they form a large quilt.

7. Display the quilt in the hall under a banner that reads, MANY CULTURES, ONE WORLD.

~ Culture Quilt Template ~

- Use creative lettering to write your name and the name of your country in the center of the template.
- In the eight outer sections, draw pictures or designs that relate to the country's culture.
- Make your designs in repetitive patterns so each section looks like a piece of fabric.
- Cut out the quilt panel and wait for your teacher's instructions.

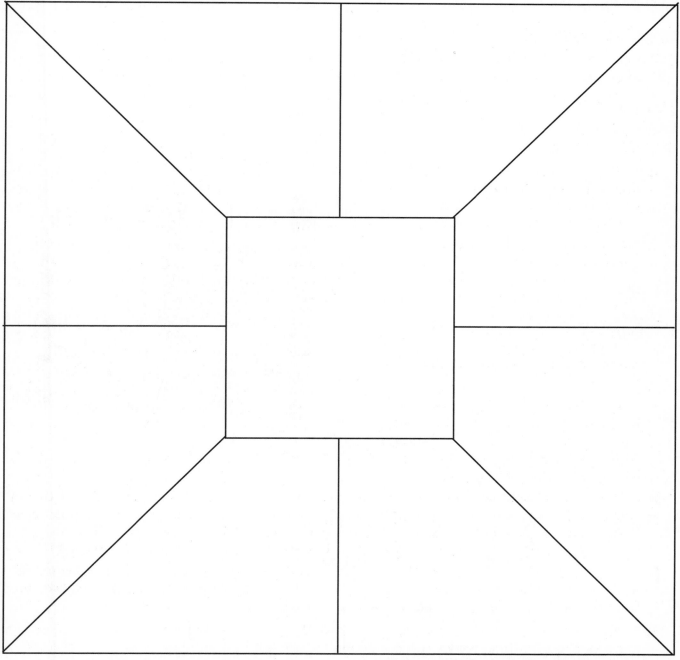

Country Report Projects for Any Country Scholastic Teaching Resources

∼ FLORAL FAN-FOLD FILE ∽

Student "botanists" will learn about the indigenous flora of different countries and keep their facts organized with this handy, free-standing display.

Materials
- copies of the File Cards template (page 49)
- colored markers and pencils
- white copy paper
- scissors
- glue sticks

Getting Started
Show students examples of botanical prints, and then have them illustrate some of their own, spotlighting unique plant life found in other countries. (You can find books of botanical prints in your local library or search for examples on the Internet.)

How-To's

1. Give each student a sheet of white copy paper. Have students fold the paper in half along its width three times.

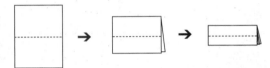

2. When they open up the paper it should reveal seven creases.

3. Ask students to fan-fold the paper along the creases.

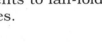

4. Have students write the title INDIGENOUS PLANT LIFE IN (NAME OF COUNTRY) across the front of the first fan-fold.

5. Give each student two copies of the File Cards template. Ask students to cut out the cards. Tell them that they will create three sets of cards that feature plants indigenous to the country they are studying. On one card they will draw a botanical print and write the plant's name. On the other card they will write a description of the plant.

6. After students have completed their cards, have them glue the first pair of cards to the front of the second fan-fold, the second pair to the third fan-fold, and the third pair to the last fan-fold. The final product should look like the example above.

7. To display the botanical prints, simply stand them up on a table or countertop. (For extra durability, this project could be constructed out of oaktag.)

~ File Cards Template ~

Botanical Print

_____

_____
_____
_____
_____
_____
_____
_____
_____

Botanical Print

_____

_____
_____
_____
_____
_____
_____
_____
_____

∿ FLAGS OF THE WORLD ∿

Integrate art into your unit by having students
create impressionistic representations of the flags of the world.

Materials
- different-colored construction paper   • glue   • pencil

Getting Started

If you want to fully integrate your study of countries across the curriculum, consider asking the art teacher to conduct this lesson. Start by showing students examples of mosaic artwork and pictures of impressionistic paintings by artists like Monet, Manet, and Seurat to illustrate how artists use swatches of different colors to create designs.

How-To's

1. Ask each student to choose a country's flag. Have students select a sheet of construction paper for each color found in the flag.

2. Have students tear off fingertip-size pieces of construction paper for each color.

3. Ask students to use a pencil to lightly sketch the design of the flag on the base sheet of construction paper.

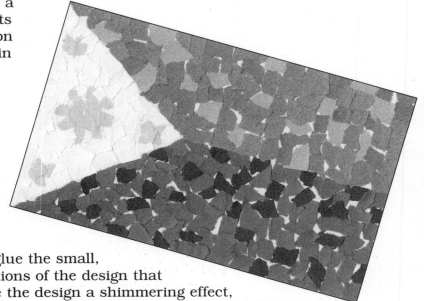

4. Then instruct students to glue the small, mosaic pieces onto the sections of the design that correspond in color. To give the design a shimmering effect, invite students to glue pieces of construction paper that are similar in color, though slightly different in value or hue, next to each other. When the viewer of the artwork stands back the colors come together to create the overall design.

5. Have students use bold lettering to write the name of the country on a strip of paper. Display the flags on a wall under each country's name, or create a border of flags near the ceiling around the classroom.

∿ Musical Instrument Poem ∿

Integrate poetry and music into your social studies curriculum by having students report on unique musical instruments from different cultures.

Materials

- colored construction paper
- colored markers and pencils
- white copy paper
- glue sticks or spray glue

Getting Started

Review poetic devices such as onomatopoeia, consonance, simile, alliteration, metaphor, assonance, and personification with your students. Show students examples of concrete poetry (also called typographical poetry or shape poetry). Explain that concrete poems are poems that are written in the shape of the object being described. For example, a poem about a garden would be written in the shape of a flower. Examples of these types of poems can be found using an Internet search engine.

Play selections of music from various cultures to give students an idea of the different sounds musical instruments can make. Discuss how music from other countries differs from the music students are used to hearing. Show the class pictures of instruments from foreign lands.

How-To's

1. Ask students to research musical instruments from different countries. Give each student a sheet of white copy paper.

2. Invite students to create a concrete poem in the shape of one of the instruments they studied. Ask them to use examples of onomatopoeia to convey the sounds of the instrument. Encourage students to write their poem in pencil in case they make a mistake. Then they should trace over the pencil with a marker and erase the pencil lines.

3. Have students create a border around the edge of the paper that relates to the country where this instrument can be found.

4. Have students glue their poem to a sheet of colored construction paper, leaving a colorful border around it.

5. Display the poems on a bulletin board under a banner that reads, POETRY IS MUSIC TO OUR EARS.

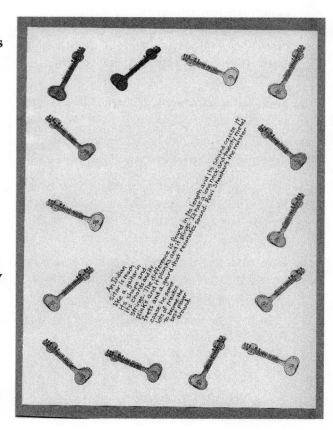

∿ FOLK TALE STORY WHEEL ∿

Expose students to different cultures by having them study tales
that have been passed down through generations.

Materials
- copies of the Story Wheel requirement sheet (page 53)
- colored markers and pencils
- large circular bowl
- scissors
- oaktag or poster board
- drafting compass

Getting Started

Review the story elements of character, setting, problem, solution, protagonist, and antagonist with your class before starting this project.

How-To's

1. Encourage students to find and read a folk tale from a foreign country.

2. Give each student a large sheet of oaktag or poster board. Have students draw their story wheels by tracing the outline of a large bowl, aluminum tray, or other circular object. Show how they can draw the circle in the center with a drafting compass or by tracing the rim of a glass or jar.

3. Next, ask students to cut out the story wheels.

4. Have students draw lines to divide the story wheel into six pie-shaped pieces.

5. Give each student a copy of the Story Wheel requirement sheet. Ask students to follow the directions to report on the folk tale they read.

6. Encourage students to use a ruler and pencil to create writing lines in each section. They can erase the pencil lines after writing the sentences in pen.

7. Display the story wheels on a bulletin board under a banner that reads, FOLK TALES FROM AROUND THE WORLD.

~ Story Wheel ~
Requirement Sheet

1 Draw a picture of the main character. Write six vivid adjectives that describe the main character around your picture.

2 Draw a picture of the setting. Describe the setting in a few complete sentences.

3 Draw a picture of the antagonist. List six vivid adjectives that describe this character.

4 Draw a picture of the main problem in the story. Write a few complete sentences that accurately describe the problem.

5 Draw a picture of the solution to the problem. Write a few complete sentences describing the solution.

6 Write a complete, detailed paragraph that describes the cultural significance of the story you chose.

Title of story

Country Report Projects for Any Country Scholastic Teaching Resources

---

Make your Story Wheel 3-D!
You can make the main character or antagonist pop up. Draw the characters on a separate sheet of paper. Draw a background on your story wheel.
Cut out the character, add tabs behind it, and glue it to the story wheel.

∾ WEATHER CIRCLE BOOK ∿

Students can compare the average temperatures of their state with those of foreign countries to gain a greater understanding of life in different regions.

Materials

- copies of the Weather Circle Book templates (pages 56–59)
- colored markers and pencils
- string
- paper clips

- scissors
- glue sticks
- thread

Getting Started

Find a Web site or reference book that charts the average monthly temperatures and annual rainfall and snowfall in your state. Print out copies for your students to use in compiling the information they will need to complete this project.

How-To's

1. Give each student a copy of the four Weather Circle Book templates.

2. On template 1, have students write a title for their weather book and draw a related illustration. They should also write their name on this page.

3. On template 2, students will compare the average monthly temperatures of their state with those of the country they're studying. Ask students to color the left box in the key one color and write the name of their state next to it. Then have them color the right box in the key a different color and write the name of the country they're studying next to that box. Have students color each pair of boxes to match the key and record the average monthly temperatures of the two places.

4. On template 3, students will graph the average annual rainfall and the average annual snowfall of their state and of the country they're studying. Have students color the key using the same colors on template 2. Then have them write numbers on the left-hand side of the graph to indicate precipitation in inches. Using the key colors, have students create a bar graph for each place that displays the average annual rainfall and snowfall of the two regions they're comparing.

5. On template 4, have students write a paragraph about a natural disaster—hurricane, typhoon, drought, earthquake, tornado, flood, volcano—that threatens the country they researched. Above the paragraph, have students draw a picture of the natural disaster. (Instead of writing about a general natural disaster, students could write about a specific occurrence that had an impact on their chosen country.)

6. After students have completed the four pages, ask them to fold the pages in half along the dashed lines and cut out the circles (figure 1).

7. Have them glue the back right side of template 1 to the back left side of template 2 (figure 2).

8. Then instruct them to glue the back right side of template 2 to the back left side of template 3. Repeat with templates 3 and 4 (figure 3).

9. To complete the circle book have students glue the back of template 4 to the back of template 1 (figure 4).

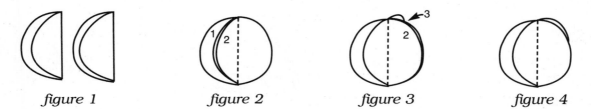

figure 1   *figure 2*   *figure 3*   *figure 4*

10. Hang a string across your classroom. Tie varying lengths of thread from the string. Tie a paper clip to the end of each piece of thread and hang the circle books from the paper clips. When a breeze blows past the circle books, they will spin and create a vibrant display of the students' work.

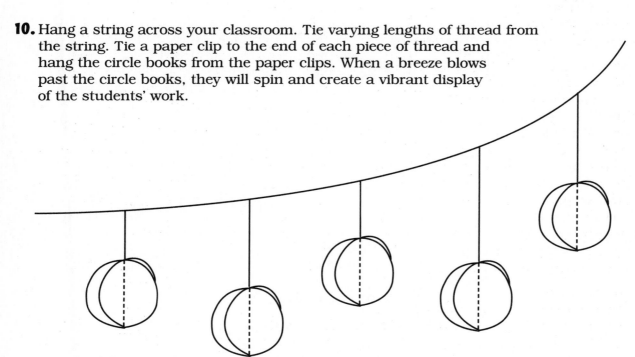

~ WEATHER BOOK TEMPLATE 1 ~
TITLE PAGE

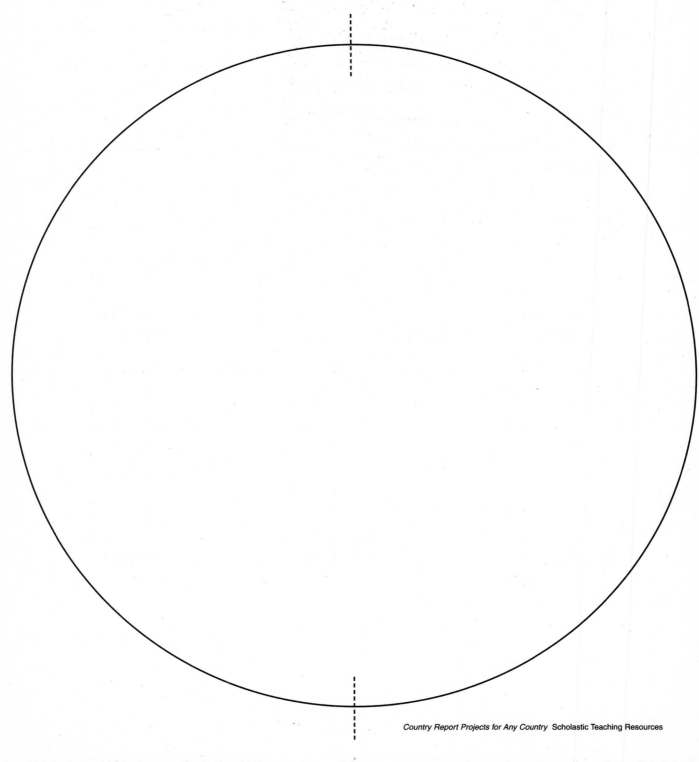

Country Report Projects for Any Country Scholastic Teaching Resources

AVERAGE TEMPERATURE

Average Temperature

Key

☐ — _____ (State)   ☐ — _____ (Country)

☐☐ **January**	☐☐ **February**

☐☐ **January**   ☐☐ **February**   ☐☐ **March**   ☐☐ **April**

☐☐ **May**   ☐☐ **June**   ☐☐ **July**   ☐☐ **August**

☐☐ **September**   ☐☐ **October**   ☐☐ **November**   ☐☐ **December**

Annual Precipitation

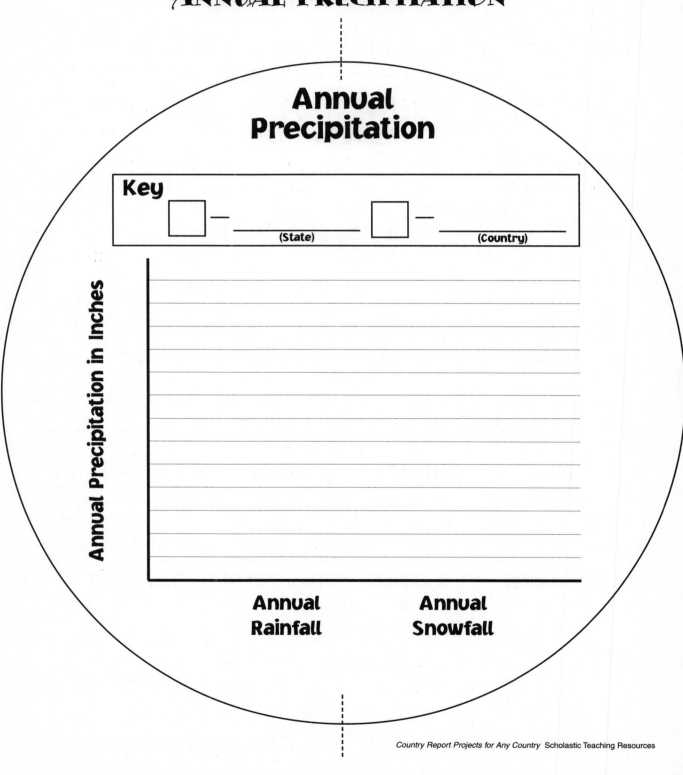

Annual Precipitation

Key

☐ — _____ (State)   ☐ — _____ (Country)

Annual Precipitation in Inches

Annual
Rainfall

Annual
Snowfall

~ Weather Book Template 4 ~
Natural Disaster

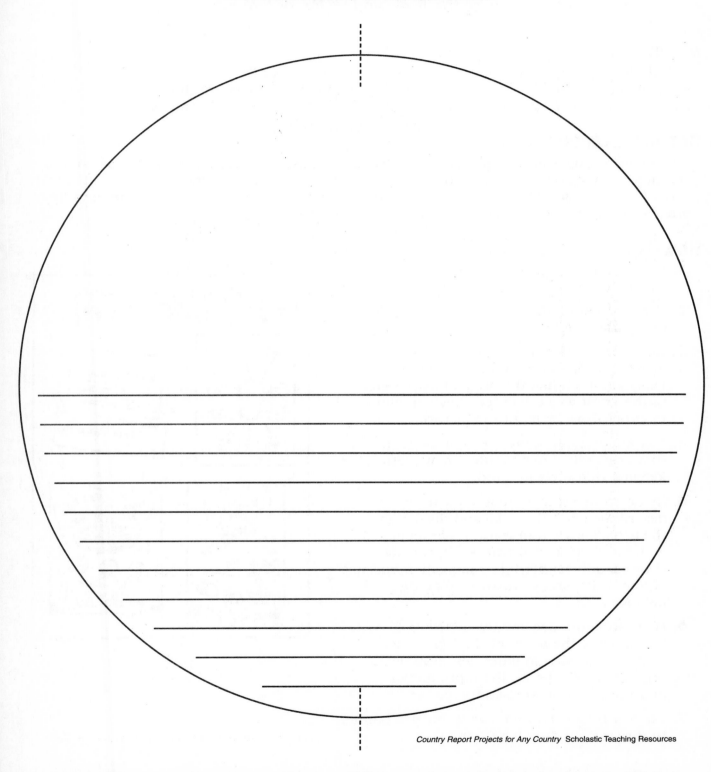

Country Report Projects for Any Country Scholastic Teaching Resources

∿ ARTISTIC REPRODUCTION ∿

Tap into the artistic intelligence of your class
as they study the lives and styles of famous artists.

Materials

- Graphic Organizer (page 61)
- construction paper
- poster boards
- glue sticks or spray glue
- various art materials (colored markers and pencils, paint, pastels, and so on)

Getting Started

Invite your school's art teacher or a knowledgeable parent to come into your classroom to conduct a lesson on art appreciation. He or she could introduce students to a variety of artists and artistic styles. Share examples of the works of artists who were influenced by other artists; show how their works are similar in style.

How-To's

1. Have students research the lives and styles of artists from different countries.

2. Give each student a copy of the Graphic Organizer to fill out.

3. Encourage students to choose one of the artist's major works and reproduce it so it looks as much like the original as possible. (If the artist was a painter, they can choose to either draw or paint the picture.)

4. Ask students to study the style of the artist they researched and create a new picture keeping that style in mind.

5. Invite students to write a letter to the artist, describing what they like and dislike about the artist's style and work. Have them address specific elements such as color choices, subject matter, composition and use of line, light, shape, texture, shading, and balance.

6. Have students use creative lettering to write the name of the artist at the top of their poster. They should glue their graphic organizer, their letter, the reproduction, and their own artwork to the poster.

7. Display the posters on a wall under a banner that reads, ARTISTIC INFLUENCES.

~ Graphic Organizer ~

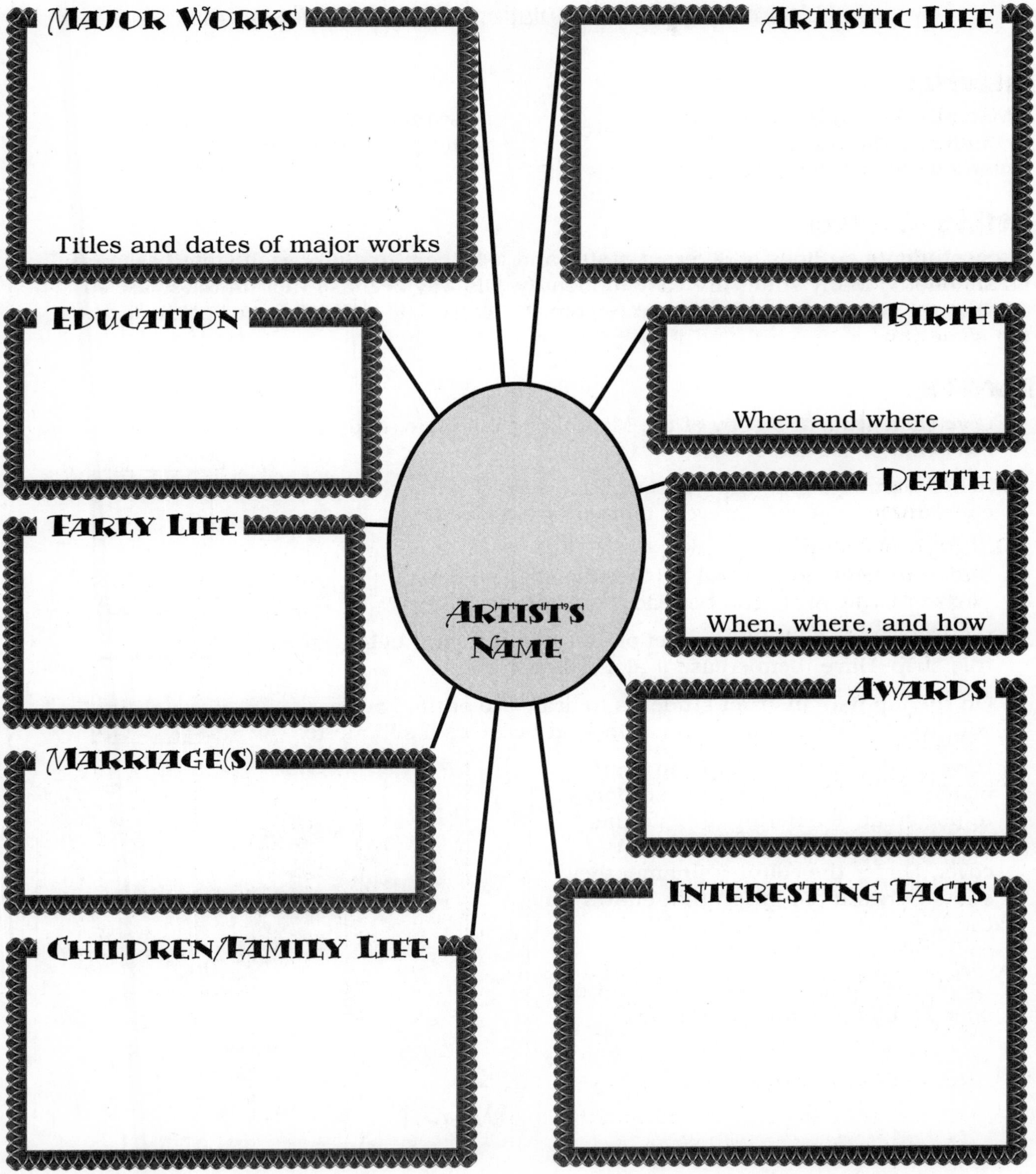

MAJOR WORKS

Titles and dates of major works

ARTISTIC LIFE

EDUCATION

BIRTH

When and where

EARLY LIFE

DEATH

When, where, and how

ARTIST'S NAME

MARRIAGE(S)

AWARDS

CHILDREN/FAMILY LIFE

INTERESTING FACTS

Country Report Projects for Any Country   Scholastic Teaching Resources

~ Country Silhouette ~

Geographic silhouettes will help students identify countries
and learn about the populations of their largest cities.

Materials

- Matchbook template (page 63)
- colored markers and pencils
- glue sticks or spray glue
- scissors
- white construction paper

Getting Started

Show students outlines of different states and ask them to guess each state based on
its silhouette. Many states are easy to identify this way because their outlines are so
distinctive. Tell students that they are going to learn to identify different countries in
the same way.

How-To's

1. Give each student a copy of the Matchbook template, and
   have him or her cut it out.

2. Ask students to glue the template to a sheet of white
   construction paper to prevent markers from bleeding
   through the paper.

3. Show students how to fold up the title strip so that
   WHAT COUNTRY AM I? can be read.

4. Have students fold the top section down and tuck it behind the
   title strip. Have them crease it along the fold.

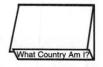

5. On the top flap, instruct students to draw the outline of the
   country they chose and shade it in so it becomes a silhouette.

6. Have students lift the flap. On the
   inside of the matchbook, tell students
   to use creative lettering to write the
   name of the country featured on the
   cover. Under the country's name, they
   should draw a bar graph that charts
   the size of the populations of the
   country's four largest cities.

7. Display the matchbooks on a bulletin
   board under a banner that reads,
   GUESS THE COUNTRIES.

WHAT COUNTRY AM I?

~ Notes ~